Hot Potatoes

Hot Potatoes

THE Collected RECIPES, Wit, AND WISDOM of WELL-KNOWN POTATO LOVERS

enid nemy

illustrated by Robert deMichiell

DOUBLEDAY

NEW YORK   LONDON   TORONTO   SYDNEY   AUCKLAND

PUBLISHED BY DOUBLEDAY
a division of Bantam Doubleday Dell Publishing Group, Inc.
666 Fifth Avenue, New York, New York 10103

DOUBLEDAY and the portrayal of an anchor with a dolphin
are registered trademarks of Doubleday,
a division of Bantam Doubleday Dell Publishing Group, Inc.

Library of Congress Cataloging-in-Publication Data
Nemy, Enid.
Hot potatoes : the collected recipes, wit, and wisdom of well-
known potato lovers / by Enid Nemy; illustrations by
Robert de Michiell.
p.   cm.
1. Cookery (Potatoes)   2. Celebrities.   3. Potatoes—Anecdotes.
I. Title.
TX803.P8N38   1993
641.6'521—dc20   92-5993
                                                    CIP

BOOK DESIGN AND ORNAMENTATION BY SIGNET M DESIGN, INC.

ISBN 0-385-46884-9

For my Mother,
Frances Nemy

CONTENTS

INTRODUCTION

THERE are all kinds of people in this world I find easy to dislike—men and women who wait until they're on the bus before digging around for change or token, the thirty-item supermarket shopper in the ten-item line, gum chewers who snap and pop, headwaiters who automatically put unknowns next to the kitchen. Still, it's occasionally possible to relate to these and other sinners of similar magnitude.

It's even possible to relate to people who don't like caviar, snails, and ice cream. But the line has to be drawn somewhere, and with me, it's at anyone who doesn't like potatoes. Actually, I believe that it's impossible not to like—no, make that love—potatoes, but I'm told there are a few such strange people, and who am I to deny that it takes all kinds . . .

It's true that the potato is ugly, but who cares. It's delicious, soothing, and comforting. It tries hard to please, even to the extent of offering itself in many varieties. As for the finished product, it's one of the few vegetables—maybe the only one—that offers a completely different taste sensation in each of its various incarnations: hot, cold, mashed, baked, boiled, roasted, fried, or scalloped—and, of course, potato chips.

It's also one of the friendliest vegetables—could it be called indiscriminating?—willing to marry or at least have an affair with any number of partners. It loves butter and sour cream, yogurt and cheese, caviar, and, to show it's not snobby, ketchup. In fact, there are few things it doesn't mate with happily.

I hope this little book will also make the potato fun to read about. The recipes are favorites of some of the country's best-known personalities. They're not difficult, they're not gourmet. They just taste good.

Hot Potatoes

THE gossip columnist for the *New York Post* and a television personality, Cindy Adams is on a first-name basis with almost every celebrity in New York City and beyond. The eightieth birthday party she gave for her husband, comedian Joey Adams, is now almost a legend, with guests such as Jackie Mason and Senator Alfonse D'Amato making toasts and Imelda Marcos singing "Happy Birthday."

"I found this recipe in an area renowned for its Lucullan haute cuisine—Las Vegas. I found it years and years ago, back when Joey was working in one of the hotel nightclubs, co-starring with Zsa Zsa Gabor, a pretty hot potato herself in those days. One day I needed something to read. Didn't find anything at hand and so I fished around in the wastebasket of my hotel suite and found a discarded Las Vegas Sun. For some reason it was turned to the food section and a page of three vegetarian dishes. One was for this gorgeous potato ragout."

CINDY'S HIGHLY DELICIOUS LOWLY POTATO RAGOUT

SERVES 6–8

6 large russet potatoes (about 3 pounds)
2 tablespoons butter
1 teaspoon Bakon yeast (available in health
  food stores. It adds nutrients, also flavor. If
  not available, go with whatever yeast you
  have.)
3 cloves garlic

3 medium onions, coarsely chopped
1 cup strong chicken (or vegetable) broth
1/2 teaspoon dried tarragon
Salt and pepper to taste
1 tablespoon olive oil
Wine vinegar
Chopped parsley

Peel and dice the potatoes. In a large skillet, heat the butter and stir in the yeast, garlic, and onions. Cook until the onions are transparent. Add the potatoes and toss to mix. When these yummy potatoes are warmed, add the broth, tarragon, and salt and pepper. Add just enough water to barely reach the top of the potatoes—not more than one cup. Let all this simmer gently for about 45 minutes, stirring often. The potatoes should be tender and most of the liquid gone. A thick sauce will form from the potato bits that fall off. Pour over this whole thing the olive oil and a little bit of wine vinegar and mix well. Sprinkle with chopped parsley. Serve piping hot.

"I adore potatoes, I eat them raw like a carrot. I dice them or slice them small and sprinkle raw in a salad."

CINDY'S BEST QUICKIE POTATO SALAD THE WORLD HAS EVER KNOWN

"**W**hen I'm desperate for a potato taste on a hot summer evening, I slice them thin, cook them fast in a pressure cooker, cool them p.d.q. in the freezer, add a hard-boiled cut-up egg, then something green—celery, peas, or green pepper—salt to taste, and mix in Miracle Whip. Not the healthy, cholesterol-free diet, lean, low-cal, or light Miracle Whip. Real Miracle Whip. Mix it up and it's the best quickie potato salad the world has ever known."

*C*hoice for best potato restaurant: "Benita's Frites, 1437 Third Street Promenade, Santa Monica, California, a little hole-in-the-wall featuring nothing but the best Belgian-style fried potatoes outside of Brussels, available with several toppings. Pray they open a branch in your hometown."—John Mariani, Esquire *magazine.*

*M*ichael Petitt, an extension agent for Boyd County in Kentucky, says that when he was a young child he'd go out with his grandmother and try to plant potatoes on the full moon. But the Old Farmer's Almanac (1991) advises that vegetables that bear crops below ground should be planted during the dark of the moon. And yet another potato grower is convinced that planting potatoes on Good Friday produces the biggest crop.

A FEW WORDS ABOUT A FEW POPULAR TYPES OF POTATOES

RUSSET BURBANK, also known as the IDAHO POTATO—brown skin, long, oval shape, better for baking and frying than boiling.

RED BLISS—round, low starch, holds shape well when boiled or sautéed. Best in spring and fall.

RED NORLAND—medium starch, oblong, available in spring.

EASTERN ROUND—light brown skin, round, medium starch, available in fall.

FINNISH POTATOES—small, round, grown principally in the Pacific Northwest—fall and winter.

BINTJE—medium-size Dutch potato, gold skin, popular in France, available in the United States.

YUKON GOLD—Canadian, dense, yellow-fleshed. Good for boiling.

LONG ISLAND KATAHDIN—somewhat waxy in texture, good for boiling.

MAINE POTATOES—good for baking.

The cradle of the potato is the Andes, where Peruvian Indians first raised them more than 5,000 years ago. The ancient method of storing them, still used in some Andean villages today, was to spread potatoes on the ground in the cold night air and follow this by several days in the sun. The villagers would then stomp on them to squeeze out the moisture the cold air and sun had not already eliminated.

Clinical studies are under way on chromium, a mineral believed to help people lose weight more easily. Chromium-rich foods include prunes, cornmeal, melon, and potatoes.

EOFFREY Beene has been described as "the quintessential designer's designer." He is the recipient of every major American fashion award, including the Coty Award (eight times), the Council of Fashion Designers of America Special Award for Fashion as Art, and the Neiman-Marcus Award. He has had museum retrospectives in New York, Cleveland, and Tokyo and his name has been institutionalized in crossword puzzles in the *New York Times* and *Newsday*. His avocations are orchid growing and collecting Art Deco drawings, paintings, and objects. His clients include Glenn Close, Claudette Colbert, Jeane Kirkpatrick, Jacqueline Kennedy Onassis, and Sigourney Weaver.

DOWN-UNDER POTATO CASSEROLE

(courtesy of Mr. Beene's sister, Barbara Wellman, who acquired the recipe in Perth, Western Australia—from an American friend)

SERVES 6

5 medium-size Idaho potatoes
1 (8-ounce) carton sour cream
1 (8-ounce) package cream cheese, at room
   temperature
1¹/₂ cups grated Cheddar cheese
Grated onion (optional—can be added if
   desired)

3 tablespoons butter or margarine (more or
   less, as desired)
¹/₂ teaspoon salt
¹/₂ teaspoon black pepper ("I use fresh
   ground.")
Milk, if needed

Preheat the oven to 350°. Grease a 1¹/₂-quart casserole.

Peel, pare, boil, drain, and mash the potatoes. Add the sour cream and cream cheese and mix well. Add 1 cup of grated Cheddar cheese (reserving ¹/₂ cup for the topping), the onion, if using it, the butter or margarine, salt, and pepper. Mix well. If too thick, add a little milk, but do not let the mixture get too thin. Place the potato mixture in the casserole. Top with the remaining ¹/₂ cup Cheddar cheese. Cover and cook for 30 to 35 minutes.

Michael Thomas, columnist, talking about a society columnist's list of top people in Long Island's fashionable Hamptons: "a roughly 100-square-mile area in which the preponderance of the land is occupied by potatoes—considered by many of us to be possibly more intelligent and indubitably more mannerly than many of the human spuds" on the list.

ELEN Gurley Brown is a woman of contrasts. She's small, as slim as a pencil on a diet, and anything but voluptuous; she's also the woman who wrote the still-famous 1962 book *Sex and the Single Girl*, and who has guided *Cosmopolitan* magazine, and its sexy, eye-catching covers, for more than twenty-five years. She's a dedicated feminist but has no hesitancy in admitting that she caters to her husband, David Brown, who co-produced such films as *The Sting*, *Jaws, The Verdict*, and *Cocoon*. She lives in a luxurious Manhattan apartment, mingles with the most glamorous names on both coasts, constantly appears on talk and interview shows, received a wildly expensive car as a thank-you gift from her publisher—and takes the bus to work. If and when she does take a taxi, she's apt to startle drivers who look in their mirrors by doing facial exercises. There's a chair in journalism in her name at Northwestern University, she's in the Publishing Hall of Fame—and she has debated at Oxford. Never mind who won.

Mrs. Brown says that although she knows potatoes are nutritious and not caloric if not loaded with extras, she's in love with rice. She does, however, prepare them for her husband, David, and as a child did have a love affair with them.

"Between the ages of ten and fourteen, my best friend, Elizabeth Jessup, and I used to each take a potato to the woods near my house in Little Rock, build a fire (we were both Girl Scouts) and bake the potatoes in the ashes. While we waited for them to be almost done enough to eat—they never got all the way cooked through—we would climb a large oak tree, evaluate the current crop of men in our lives, discuss Mr. Curry, our saturnine but attractive math teacher, and plan for the future.

"This was in the midst of the Depression and potatoes, tree, and friendship brought a whole lot of enjoyment (and nutrition) for about five cents per girl (including the matches) and got us out of our family's hair for hours. Listen, I'm getting turned on just thinking about those potatoes. I may go bake one right now."

HELEN'S STUFFED POTATO SKINS

Baking potatoes
Low-fat cottage cheese
Low-fat yogurt

Low-cal salad dressing
Lemon juice
Green onion, chopped

Bake the whole potatoes for 1 hour at 350°. Turn off the oven and let the potatoes remain in it for another hour. Scoop out all the insides. Use them for potato salad or eat them while you work.

Do a mixture of cottage cheese, yogurt, salad dressing, and lemon juice, the amount based on the number of skins. Line the skins with this mixture, about $^3/_4$ inch thick. Put tons of chopped green onion on top. Serve quickly while the skins are still warm.

THINK of "Diamonds Are a Girl's Best Friend" and "Hello, Dolly" and one person comes to mind—Carol Channing, a musical comedy star who has been illuminating every branch of American theater for some forty years. Her performances in *Gentlemen Prefer Blondes* and *Hello, Dolly*, her one-woman show, and her tour with Mary Martin, broke theater records everywhere. She's been in numerous films, won Tony and Emmy awards, and been nominated for an Oscar. One of her best friends is Betty White, the unforgettable Sue Ann Nivens of "The Mary Tyler Moore Show" and, more recently, one of the "Golden Girls." Ms. White has won five Emmy Awards, has made several television movies, and in 1990 received the Lifetime Achievement Award on the American Comedy Awards.

Carol Channing: "I am a potato lover but I pale into insignificance compared to my dear friend Betty White. I well remember dining with Betty at the legendary Chasen's restaurant in Beverly Hills. Betty, as usual, ordered a side dish of French-fried potatoes, but as Maude Chasen, the proprietess, is a close friend of Betty's, she saw to it that there was a huge tureen of her special French fries as a centerpiece. Unfortunately, Betty was called back to the studio for additional shooting on the 'Golden Girls' and couldn't finish her potatoes. I had a special messenger bring them to her home. Late that night, she phoned to say she'd not only finished shooting, but had finished off the French fries—and went on to rhapsodize about the glories of feasting on potatoes."

FAVORITE POTATO RECIPE

(given to Betty White by her mother)

SERVES 4

4 large baking potatoes
Fresh parsley, chopped
Freshly grated Parmesan cheese
$^1/_2$ teaspoon dried thyme leaves

$^1/_4$ cup butter or margarine, melted
$^1/_4$ cup salad oil
$^1/_2$–1 teaspoon salt

Preheat the oven to 400°.

Cut the unpared potatoes into $^1/_4$-inch slices. Place overlapping slices (about half the potatoes) in an oiled oven-to-table baking dish.

Cover with half the chopped parsley, grated cheese, and melted butter. Sprinkle with thyme and salt. Top with the remaining potato slices, then the other half of the cheese, parsley, and butter.

Bake for 30 minutes, or until the potatoes are done and browned at the edges. Serve immediately.

A Peter Duchin band lends a certain cachet to social events; Peter Duchin there in person, playing the piano and leading the band, is status. The son of the pianist and bandleader Eddy Duchin, Peter was raised by Governor Averell Harriman of New York and Mrs. Harriman in an ambiance of privilege and power, and for years he practiced some pretty fancy footwork to maintain his bachelor status. He is now married to Brooke Hayward, the author of *Haywire*, and although both have the credentials for society's so-called A lists, they're rarely seen at the glitz and glitter events that keep four and five Duchin bands playing nightly during the season. Mr. Duchin himself plays about a hundred engagements a year, but when it's time off, both he and his wife prefer quiet dinners and good conversation with a few friends. Can't afford a Duchin band? Not to worry. Dance to one of the many Duchin albums, or put on a video of *Working Girl* and catch a glimpse.

POTATOES AU GRATIN

SERVES 6

1 tablespoon soft butter
1 clove garlic, crushed
6 medium-size Idaho potatoes
1 cup coarsely grated Gruyère cheese

Salt and freshly ground pepper to taste
1 cup half and half
$^1/_4$ teaspoon freshly ground nutmeg

Preheat the oven to 375°. Rub a 10-inch gratin dish with butter and garlic.

Peel and slice the potatoes paper thin. Divide the potatoes into three parts and layer in the gratin dish, sprinkling Gruyère, salt, and pepper between each layer, ending with Gruyère. Pour half and half over all gently, and sprinkle nutmeg on the top.

Place uncovered in the oven for 45 minutes to 1 hour, until the potatoes are done. These can be done ahead of time and reheated. They are excellent as an accompaniment to all roast meats and fish.

According to Consumer Reports, *regular potato chips, made of sliced potatoes, oil, and salt, get 60 percent of their calories from fat but have little saturated fat and no cholesterol. Kettle-style chips, hand cooked and with thicker slices, are crunchier than regular and may look oily but often have less fat. Fabricated chips, made from a dough of dried potato flakes, are more uniform but may have sugar, corn, wheat, colors, and preservatives.*

According to an article in Natural History by Raymond Sokolov, *the sweet potato ranks second in the world, after the potato, among root and tuber crops, and China now produces 80 percent of all the sweet potatoes worldwide. In China, sweet potatoes are used in the manufacture of liquor, vinegar, plastics, synthetic rubber, artificial fiber, and color film.*

ATHIE Lee Gifford has a lot to be grateful for, but still—how can she be so perky so consistently so early in the morning? Well, whatever her secret, it is just one of the ingredients that have led to the success of the nationally syndicated television program "Live with Regis and Kathie Lee."

There may be other secrets as well, but basically, there isn't much about Kathie Lee that isn't known to viewers. Her marriage to Frank Gifford, the sportscaster, her pregnancy, the birth of her son, Cody Newton, have all been the subjects of unrehearsed, unscripted conversation and banter with co-host Regis Philbin. Although she shot into television prominence within the last decade, Kathie Lee has been in show business for almost twenty-five years. In addition to her daily program, she's seen on commercials and for several years has had a nightclub act with Mr. Philbin. The latest in a mind-boggling series of activities was co-hosting with Regis the 1992 Miss America contest.

Perhaps because of these mind-boggling activities, Kathie Lee doesn't spend a lot of time in front of a stove. The following recipe is a family favorite, provided by her sister, Michelle Mader, for the "Live" Newsletter.

SWEET POTATO SOUFFLÉ

SERVES 8—10

3 pounds sweet potatoes, peeled, cooked, and
    mashed (Hint: the smaller they are cut up,
    the smoother they will whip up.)
2 eggs
3/4 cup brown sugar

1/2 cup butter, melted
1 teaspoon cinnamon
1 teaspoon salt
Orange juice—up to 1 cup
1 cup pecan halves for topping

Preheat the oven to 375°.

Using an electric mixer at medium speed, beat into the potatoes the eggs with 1/4 cup of the brown sugar and 1/4 cup of melted butter (the remaining 1/4 cup of each of these ingredients will be used for the topping).

Now add the cinnamon and salt and 2 tablespoons of the orange juice. Beat until fluffy, adding additional orange juice as needed to fluff and/or moisten. When desired consistency is reached, place the mixture into a 2-quart casserole, cover the top with pecans, sprinkle with the remaining brown sugar and drizzle butter over this topping. Bake uncovered for 20 minutes.

Try a hint of coconut in sweet potato recipes.

LAINE Kaufman opened Elaine's restaurant in 1963 and since that time has become den mother to half of New York City's literary establishment as well as visiting literary figures and a good percentage of movie stars, writers, directors, and agents. On any given night, the patrons range from Woody Allen and Michael Caine to Alan King, Alan Pakula, Gay Talese, and Mario Puzo. It's been said that for a "regular" to be turned away would be as traumatic as being turned out in the snow by one's mother.

"I live a party life," says Elaine. "Elsa Maxwell used to have to send out invitations. I just open the door."

SFORMATO DI PATATE

"Years ago, I was having dinner in Rome with Jason Robards, Lauren Bacall, Sidney Chaplin, and Lionel Stander, and a cast of many who were shooting a spaghetti western. After many courses, we were served a potato mold, garnished with artichokes. It turned out to be the same dish my mother made at holidays."

SERVES 6

1 pound potatoes, peeled
$^1/_2$ pound butter
Salt and pepper
$^1/_4$ cup grated Parmesan cheese

3 eggs, separated
Small, cooked artichokes, quartered, for garnish

Preheat the oven to 350°. Butter a 10-inch mold.

Boil the potatoes and puree through a sieve. Combine with the butter, salt, pepper, cheese, and egg yolks. Fold in stiffly beaten egg whites. Turn into the buttered mold. Set in a pan of boiling water that comes halfway up the sides of the mold. Bake in the preheated oven for about 20 minutes. Garnish with the artichokes.

James Beard liked potatoes baked at 450° for 2 hours. Before baking, prick with the tines of a fork; when done cut lengthwise and across the middle but not quite through. Mash with a fork and add freshly ground black pepper. Optional additions: butter, salt, or yogurt.

Old American cookbooks frequently suggest adding mashed potatoes to cake batter. Although it may sound heavy, it produces a lighter cake. A general proportion is 1 cup mashed potatoes to 1$^3/_4$ cups sifted cake flour, adding the mashed potatoes to the butter, sugar, and egg mixture.

EDWARD I. KOCH

ALWAYS colorful and controversial, Ed Koch served three terms (1978–1989) as the 105th Mayor of the City of New York. He had previously been a congressman for nine years, a City Council member for two, and a sergeant with the 104th Infantry division during World War II. A graduate of New York University Law School, he is now a partner in the law firm of Robinson Silverman Pearce Aronsohn & Berman.

"When I was young, my mother made potato latkes. The secret was to deep-fry them in chicken fat. Such a latke is truly the most delicious one you will ever have, particularly if served with a dollop of applesauce. If the meal is dairy, then a dollop of sour cream can be substituted.

"You have to understand that if you are not acclimated to chicken fat cooking, which occurs only over a period of years, it can kill you. Death is never instantaneous. It takes a large number of latkes eaten over a large number of years, but every step of the way is filled with pleasure.

"People don't use chicken fat anymore, and chickens have been genetically altered so that they don't produce the fat that they used to.

"The best crispy cottage potatoes, regrettably fried in some uninteresting oil instead of chicken fat, à la carte and very expensive, can be found at Ben Benson's restaurant. But you can't die from their potatoes—I think."

KOCH POTATO LATKES

Grate raw potatoes until they become pulp. Drain the water from the pulp. (Do not drink it—it tastes terrible, believe me.)

Add chopped onions—roughly 2 percent of the mix.

Use 2 eggs for 35 latkes: add the yolks directly and the whites after beating stiff. Shape the latkes like croquettes—not too large, not too small. Then add salt and pepper.

Deep-fry in chicken fat.

One of the most exclusive beers in the country is Spud Premier, produced in Wisconsin in late summer and available for only six to eight weeks each year. The beer, made by Wisconsin's Stevens Point Brewery, situated in the potato-farming area, has potato starch in place of corn as one of its ingredients. It was made originally, and still is, to coincide with the Spud Bowl, a university fund raiser held at the end of September.

The potato has nowhere to go but up, according to Ash DeLorenzo, trend director of Brain Reserve, Inc., in New York City. "The days of glitzy dining out are over," he says. "I see more and more orders of baked potatoes. It's part of the trend to hearty family-style, more basic food."

ANN LANDERS

ACCORDING to the 1991 *Guinness Book of World Records*, Ann Landers is the most widely syndicated columnist in the world, with an estimated readership of 90 million in over 1,200 newspapers. She has received scores of honorary degrees since she began writing her column in 1955 and was the recipient of the Citation for Distinguished Service from the American Medical Association, the highest honor given to a lay person. She has written a number of books and articles, and she lectures around the world. In private life, she is Mrs. Eppie Lederer and lives in Chicago.

"Not original but one of my favorites."

TUNA STUFFED POTATO

SERVES 1

1 large potato, baked
1 (3^1/$_2$-ounce) can water-packed tuna,
   drained
1 stalk celery, finely chopped

1 tablespoon finely chopped onion
2 tablespoons plain nonfat yogurt, or
   1 tablespoon feta cheese
1 tablespoon Dijon or other mustard

Preheat the oven to 375°.

Split the potato lengthwise and scoop out the flesh. Mix with the other ingredients. Stuff back into the potato shells. Sprinkle with ^{1}/$_2$ tablespoon Parmesan cheese if desired—or leave plain, sprinkled lightly with paprika. Bake for 15 to 20 minutes until crisp on top.

Chopped cooked vegetables may be substituted for tuna and will lower fat and caloric counts.

Chris Holmes of New Penny Farm in Presque Isle, Maine, grows eight kinds of potatoes, most of them not found anywhere else. They are harvested by hand and there are no chemical sprays. Among the varieties are yellow-fleshed Caroles and Bintjes for baking or roasting, moist Katahdins wonderful for mashed potatoes, and low-starch red-skinned Sangres for salads. A 10-pound sampler of four kinds is $25 including shipping east of the Mississippi. There is even a Potato of the Month Club. Information: New Penny Farm, 85 Williams Road, Presque Isle, Me 04769; (207) 768–7551.

NO-WORK LOW-FAT UNFRIED FRIES

(from Miss Landers' daughter, Margo Howard)

Preheat the oven to 450°.

Slice an Idaho baker lengthwise into 3 or 4 slices, depending on whether it's a medium or large potato. You can use a tiny bit of olive oil, or not, then sprinkle the top of each oval slice with salt and pepper. Bake for 45 minutes. The potatoes will be browned and puffed up.

V*ariations:* Sprinkle with rosemary and garlic—or any herbs you like. Can also serve with ketchup, to be like French fries.

M*eredith and E. Thomas Hughes run what they call the world's only potato museum from their home in Great Falls, Virginia. Their collection includes hundreds of historical documents and tools documenting potato production and a 4,000-year-old potato discovered in Chile. About a hundred pieces from the collection were included in the "Seeds of Change" exhibit at the National Museum of Natural History at the Smithsonian Institution in Washington. The exhibit featured five elements—potato, sugar, corn, disease, and the horse—and their impact on both the Old and the New Worlds since 1492. The museum's library and archives are available to researchers. Telephone (703) 759–6714.*

JOHN LORING'S FAVORITE POTATO-INDULGING PLACES

John Loring is Design Director of Tiffany & Co.

French fries—La Coupole, Paris

Gratin Dauphinoise—La Vagenande, Paris

Pommes Sarladaise—Aux Fins Gourmets, Paris

Pommes Soufflées—Louis XIV, Boulevard St. Denis, Paris

Pommes Purées—Brasserie Lipp, Paris

Potato Pancakes—The Post House, New York City

New Potatoes Sautéed with Rosemary—La Collina Pistoiese, Milan

---

Alan Fairweather, an Edinburgh botanist, by his own reckoning eats 4 to 5 pounds of potatoes daily, according to The Wall Street Journal. *Mr. Fairweather apparently likes them "boiled in their own jackets" and has a Victorian study crammed with such publications as* Potato News *and* The History and Social Influence of the Potato.

Store potatoes in a cool, dry, dark, well-ventilated area. At 45° to 50° potatoes will keep for several weeks; at room temperature for one week.

Don't refrigerate potatoes—that will result in a sweet taste as the starch turns to sugar.

Don't expose to sunlight or artificial light—that will cause potatoes to acquire a bitter flavor.

Make any recipe of spiced nuts, preferably with pecans, and, using some cayenne pepper, chop not too fine. Fold into sweet potatoes mashed with milk and butter.

S Robin Leach might say, it's just his glass of champagne, mingling with the rich and famous, exploring how they live and what makes them tick and, in the process, amassing a tidy little fortune (or maybe it's a big one, the figures aren't public). Even as a teenager in England, Mr. Leach had defined his priorities—"there has always been something about the biggest, the wealthiest, the best known, the most prestigious, that has appealed to me," he recalled—and happily, some years later, millions of television viewers agreed.

Mr. Leach, who came to New York in 1963 (and sold shoes in a Fifth Avenue store), held a variety of news and television jobs before the 1983 launch of "Lifestyles of the Rich and Famous," a peek into the private lives and homes of celebrities, millionaires, and moguls. "Runaway with the Rich and Famous" followed. The programs and other diverse activities add up to more than 250,000 miles of travel a year, a figure that gives new meaning to the term "frequent flyer."

RICH AND FAMOUS BAKED POTATOES

As many potatoes as people to be served
Sour cream
Parmesan cheese, grated

Pepper
Caviar

Bake the potatoes at 350°. Halve the potatoes and scoop the pulp into a blender or food processor.

For each portion, add 1 ounce sour cream, 2 tablespoons grated Parmesan cheese, and a pinch of pepper. Blend or process and return to the potato shells.

Cover generously with caviar. Pop a cork and have a glass of bubbly.

THE CHOMPER AND THE POTATO CHIP ART

(September 1990)

FORT WAYNE, Ind. (AP)—A man visiting a retirement expo spotted what looked like a tray of free samples of potato chips, so he took one and started to chew—and nearly broke Myrtle Young's heart.

Young, 66, had long ago started a collection of potato chips that resemble famous people, animals and objects when she was a chip inspector at Seyfert's Foods Inc. She and her chips have appeared on "Late Night with David Letterman" and "The Tonight Show."

On Saturday, she had about 75 chips on display, including one that looked like a perfect sand dollar.

"I saw chips laying there as samples, so I picked one up," recalled Gregory Hough of Fort Wayne.

He was quickly collared by a salesperson for Seyfert's and ordered to spit out what remained of the sand-dollar chip, which had been masticated beyond salvage.

QUITE a number of women, and men for that matter, have style. Very few have the distinctive style of Paloma Picasso, a woman at once both dramatic (trademark red, red, red lips outlined against a pale, almost translucent complexion) and elegant (she is almost a fixture on the International Best Dressed List). The daughter of Pablo Picasso and Françoise Gilot, who is now Mrs. Jonas Salk, Miss Picasso was born and educated in Paris and began her design career in 1969 when Yves St. Laurent presented a collection of her jewelry. She has designed gold jewelry for Zolotas as well, and in 1980 began an association with Tiffany's. She has since branched out into other areas, including handbags and perfume, and as her own best model is one of the most recognizable faces in fashion.

"When I was a little girl, I would spend a lot of time in the South of France, and in the summertime it would get extremely hot. The gardener would get potatoes and slice them and put the slices on my face and temples to cool me down.

"Grated potato is good on burns. It absorbs the heat and leaves the area feeling cool.

"Grated, fresh raw potatoes are also great to help bring down a fever. Grate raw potatoes, gather them in a bunch in your hand, and lay them on your forehead. After a while the potatoes absorb the heat. Once they become warm, continue with a fresh bunch."

PALOMA POTATO SANDWICH

"I always thought the combination of potatoes and lettuce was delicious. So I invented my own sandwich.

"Line French baguette bread with lettuce, olive oil, and vinaigrette dressing. Pour on a puree of potatoes. A great sandwich."

Kyle MacLachlan, one of the stars of the still-remembered "Twin Peaks" television series, filmed four commercials for potato chips in England (the British call chips "crisps"). According to People magazine, the script called for MacLachlan to describe them as "damn fine crisps," but a British advertising regulatory group decided that "damn" would offend young viewers. The Solomon-like judgment was "darn fine crisps" for commercials airing before 9 P.M. and "damn fine" after that hour.

New Potatoes en Papillote: Scrape off the skins, place on foil or parchment, add a chunk of butter, a little salt, and some mint—fresh, if possible. Bake in a 400° oven for 35 minutes.

One pound of fresh potatoes equals about 3 medium potatoes, 3 cups peeled and sliced, or 2 cups mashed.

ANNA QUINDLEN

A 1974 graduate of Barnard College and a member of the college's Board of Trustees, Anna Quindlen joined the *New York Times* in 1977 as a general assignment reporter and later became the paper's deputy Metropolitan editor. She created the column "Life in the 30's" and now writes "Public and Private," which appears twice weekly on the Op Ed page and is syndicated to newspapers throughout the country. She is married to Gerald Krovatin, an attorney, and is the mother of three children.

When her second son, Christopher, was four years old, he confined his eating to chicken, cheese, pasta, and anything from McDonald's and announced that he did not like potatoes, Ms. Quindlen said.

"My heart sank because as a matter of policy, I have decided I have nothing in common with people who don't like potatoes, just as I have nothing in common with people who don't like fettuccine Alfredo or brownies," she continued.

"But his older brother, Quindlen, butted in and saved the day. 'French fries are potatoes, Christopher,' he said. 'And home fries are potatoes. And potato chips. And mashed potatoes.'

" 'Oh,' Christopher replied. 'Then I do like potatoes after all.'

"Whew!

"Then they told their favorite joke: What does a frog eat with his hamburger? Answer: French flies."

ANNA QUINDLEN'S COUCH POTATO

SERVES 1

1 Idaho potato
Olive oil
Butter
Sour cream with chives

Freshly ground black pepper
Sharp Cheddar cheese, grated (optional)
Salt

Preheat the oven to 350°.

Rub the potato with olive oil, prick with a fork, and bake for 1 hour.

Squish the potato to make an opening at the top. Fill with the butter, sour cream with chives, freshly ground pepper, and grated Cheddar cheese, if you wish. Just butter will do. Salt well.

Eat in front of the television, preferably while watching a nighttime soap or an old movie with Tracy and Hepburn.

Eat the potato skin because it's good for you and tastes good.

THAT'S to say about Joan Rivers that isn't already known? Her adventures with Johnny Carson and the Fox network? Not news. Her "wonderdog" Spike? Not news. Devoted mother, inexhaustible energy, fierce determination—we know! She's the author of several books and host of a talk show; when she isn't appearing at Las Vegas or Lake Tahoe or Atlantic City, she's on stage for various charities. She's been in films, on Broadway, and honored with the Harvard Hasty Pudding Woman of the Year and Harvard Instant Pudding Award as well as what appear to be several hundred others. And her signature question "Can we talk?" is a registered federal trademark. Something you might not know—she's much lower-keyed in private life—but equally as quick with one-liners, barbed and otherwise.

"The best potatoes on the entire planet are the French fries at the original Nathan's in Coney Island, Brooklyn. They're greasy. They're great. They're the reason God said, 'And let there be ketchup!'"

JOAN RIVERS' BELTED NEW POTATOES

SERVES 4

20 small, red new potatoes
1 stick sweet butter
2 tablespoons minced dried or fresh dill
1–2 teaspoons garlic powder
$^1/_2$ teaspoon salt

Mixed black and green fresh pepper (8–10
  turns of the peppermill)
Pinches of parsley, sage, rosemary, and thyme
  (optional)

Wash and scrub the potatoes thoroughly. Peel a thin strip of skin from around the center of each potato.

Drop the potatoes into 2 quarts of rapidly boiling water and cook, uncovered, for 10 minutes. Drain and set aside.

Return the empty pot to the stove and, over low flame, melt the butter.

Return the potatoes to the pot and add the remaining ingredients. Cover the pot and shake vigorously.

Cook over low flame for 10 minutes, or until the potatoes are tender, shaking the pan frequently so the potatoes don't stick. Serve surrounding a roast, in a chafing dish, or on a platter garnished with parsley or radicchio.

New Potatoes: Boil until tender. Remove the skins. Roll in melted butter and (a) chopped nuts or (b) lemon juice combined with grated lemon rind and chopped fresh chives.

NOWN as Andrew to his good friends, Andy Rooney spent the first fifty years of his career trying to attract attention to his writing and the last ten trying to avoid the attention he's attracted from his commentaries on "60 Minutes." That's what he claims on the jacket of his own book *Not That You Asked.*

"When dinner is over and I disappear into the kitchen, my guests invariably start chatting incoherently in anxious anticipation of what I've prepared for dessert.

"Although I hesitate to select one potato recipe as my best, I must say I get a great many favorable comments on my potato ice cream."

ANDY ROONEY'S POTATO ICE CREAM

(Do not serve to guests who are calorie conscious.)

SERVES ABOUT 6

4 large Idaho potatoes
1¹/₄ cups granulated sugar
6 cups water

2 cups heavy cream
Dash of paprika
Any good chocolate sauce

Peel the potatoes, setting the peels aside. Cut the potatoes lengthwise into ¹/₂-inch slices. Discard the rounded top and bottom slices. Place a stack of slices, which now have a flat surface, on a cutting board and slice them again, producing long fingers. Turn these parallel to the cutting-board edge and slice them once more into small cubes.

Add the sugar to the water and simmer the potato cubes until the water evaporates. (Mr. Rooney says his method is until one of the cubes adheres to a single chopstick.)

Place the cooked potatoes in a blender with the cream and a dash of paprika for color, and blend well.

Pour the potato mixture into a divided ice-cube tray and place in the freezer (another Rooney aside—"if you have a microwave freezer, all the better"). When the mixture begins to thicken, but before it hardens, insert a toothpick into each cube and continue freezing. (The toothpick should stand upright.) When the toothpick no longer pulls out easily, the ice cream cubes are ready.

Plan on 3 cubes per guest and serve with a bowl of rich chocolate sauce for dipping. Only after dinner, says Mr. Rooney, should you throw out the potato peels. Don't ask why.

*O*ne of the country's leading food writers and critics, Ms. Sheraton was born into a family where food was important, and cooking and sampling became her hobby. She has taken courses at Le Cordon Bleu in Paris and private lessons in Chinese, Lebanese, Thai, Turkish, Danish, and Vietnamese cookery. She has written for numerous magazines, including *New York*, *Time*, and *Vanity Fair*, was with the *New York Times* for eight years, and is now food editor of *Condé Nast Traveler*. Her latest book is *Mimi Sheraton's Favorite New York Restaurants*.

"Because the necessary ingredients for this soup were staples, my mother could cook this up whenever she decided that her main course was a bit skimpy. Invariably, we all ate so much of it that we never touched what followed."

POTATO SOUP

MAKES ABOUT 1 1/2 QUARTS

3 or 4 large boiling potatoes (about 1 1/4
    pounds), peeled
5–6 cups water
3 stalks celery, diced
Celery leaves
3 sprigs parsley, preferably the Italian variety
3 sprigs dill

1 small carrot, scraped
1/2 teaspoon salt
1/8 teaspoon white pepper, or to taste
2 1/2 tablespoons sweet butter
2 tablespoons diced onion
2 1/2 tablespoons flour
1/4 teaspoon thyme

Cut the peeled raw potatoes into approximately 1/2-inch cubes. Place in a 3-quart stainless-steel or enameled soup pot and add the water, which should cover, do not add more than 6 cups. Add the celery. If you do not mind bits of leaves floating in the soup, do as my mother did and add them coarsely chopped. If you do not like them in the soup, leave them on the stalks, so they can be picked out when the soup is done. Add the parsley, dill, carrot, salt, and pepper. Bring to a boil, skimming off scum as it rises to the surface, and when the soup is clear, cover and reduce to a slow but steady simmer. Cook until the potatoes are tender but not falling apart, about 15 minutes. Remove the parsley and dill. Keep the soup simmering gently.

In a small saucepan, heat the butter; when it bubbles add the diced onion. Sauté slowly, stirring frequently, until the onion becomes light golden brown. Stir in the flour and sauté until it becomes cocoa brown. Stir in about 1/2 cup of soup liquid to this roux (einbrenne), then beat the mixture into the simmering soup. Add the thyme. Increase the heat to just below a boil and stir until the einbrenne is completely absorbed. Simmer for 10 to 15 minutes. Check the seasoning and serve.

CLAM AND POTATO CHOWDER

Follow the above recipe exactly, but add 10 large chowder clams. Trim the hard parts from the soft parts, and add their liquor to the water with the raw potatoes. Add the soft sections of the clams after 20 minutes.

CHOCOLATE POTATO TORTE

(Schokoladen-Kartoffeltorte)

3–4 medium-size baking potatoes (or 1³/₄
*   cups cooked, finely mashed potatoes)*
4 eggs, separated
2 ounces (squares) bitter chocolate
¹/₂ teaspoon baking powder
2 cups sifted flour

1 cup ground unblanched almonds
³/₄ cup butter
1²/₃ cups sugar
2 teaspoons vanilla extract
1 tablespoon sugar

If possible, boil and peel the potatoes a day ahead of time so they can dry out a little. If not, be sure they are thoroughly cold before you mash them or they will stick together and be difficult to blend evenly into the batter. For best results, puree the potatoes through a food mill, sieve, or ricer. Measure off 1³/₄ cupfuls and set aside. Preheat the oven to 350°. Separate the eggs so the whites will not be too cold when you beat them. Melt the chocolate over hot water. Add the baking powder to the flour and sift again, together, onto a sheet of paper.

Add almonds to the flour and gently toss together with a fork until thoroughly blended. Cream the butter with 1²/₃ cups sugar until light and fluffy. Beat in the egg yolks and when blended, beat in the melted chocolate, potatoes, and vanilla. Whip the egg whites and as they begin to stiffen, beat in the 1 tablespoon sugar. Continue beating until whites stand in stiff but glossy peaks. Beat 2 or 3 tablespoons of the stiffened egg whites into the chocolate batter to lighten it. Turn the egg whites into a wide, roomy bowl, unless they are already in one. Turn the chocolate batter onto the egg whites, and sprinkle with the flour-nut mixture. Using a rubber spatula, fold the egg whites, chocolate batter, and flour together, gently but thoroughly. There should be no traces of flour or egg white showing.

Bake in two unbuttered 9-inch layer cake pans or in an 8-inch springform. In a layer cake pan, this takes about 40 minutes, in a springform, about 50 minutes. When the cake is done, a tester inserted in the middle should come out clean. Cool in the pan, invert onto a rack until completely cold. If you have used a springform, cut the cake into two layers. The layers may be filled with whipped cream, or chocolate butter cream.

In its purest form, a medium 5-ounce potato provides only 155 calories and is virtually free of fat and sodium.

More than 500 million pounds of frozen French fries were produced for retail sale in 1988.

When buying processed French fries, a good guide is the larger the cut of the fry, the lower its fat content. Smaller cuts, like shoestrings, absorb more oil.

BOBBY SHORT

OBBY Short describes himself as a saloon pianist and singer. Perhaps more accurate are the *Newsweek* and *Time* magazine descriptions: "a collector's item," according to one, and "the very symbol of elegance and style," according to the other. Mr. Short is now (1992) in his twenty-fifth year at New York's most rarified of cabarets, the Café Carlyle, and his interpretations of the songs of Cole Porter, George Gershwin, Rodgers and Hart, Irving Berlin, Stephen Sondheim, and other important composers at nightclubs in New York, Hollywood, Paris, and London have attracted fans as varied as the Duke and Duchess of Windsor, Eugene McCarthy, and Leontyne Price. He's been a frequent performer at the White House for Presidents Nixon, Carter, and Reagan, and his career has included two concerts with Mabel Mercer, appearances with the Boston and New York Pops, and with symphony orchestras across the country.

"I grew up in Danville, Illinois, during the Depression and we ate potatoes a lot. And when we had a cold, goose grease would be massaged on our chest—it was never used for cooking, as the

French do. When I went to live in France, as a young entertainer, the two—potatoes and goose grease—finally got together, with magical results."

POTATOES L'AMI BOBBY SHORT

(courtesy of George Huycke)

Potatoes
Duck or goose fat
Garlic, chopped

Salt and pepper
Parsley, chopped

Parboil, then peel and slice the potatoes. Melt duck or goose fat in an iron skillet. Add garlic and the potatoes, season with salt and pepper, and fry the potatoes. Do not allow them to brown.

Preheat the oven to 400°.

Pack the potatoes down in the skillet with a pie tin or something with weight and place in the oven for about 15 minutes, or until the potatoes form a solid mass. Turn over, as with an upside-down cake, sprinkle with parsley, and serve.

Reduce fat by thickening sauces and soups with pureed potatoes or potato starch, instead of milk or cream.

"Someone once asked me why I said that Spencer Tracy was like a baked potato. I think it is because I think that he was very basic as an actor. He was there skins and all—in his performances. He was cooked and ready to eat."—Katharine Hepburn in Me

BEVERLY SILLS

THE word count on her career is astronomical; *The New Yorker* critic once described her as one of the wonders of New York, "way ahead of such things as the Statue of Liberty and the Empire State Building." The wonder so described is Beverly Sills, known also as "Bubbles," a coloratura soprano who went on to even greater operatic glory in the years following—a "worldwide phenomenon," said *Time* magazine. The exuberant sometime-Reubenesque redhead—warm, good-humored, breezy, outspoken, irreverent—also spent almost a decade as general director of the New York City Opera. One of the comparatively few artists with financial and fund-raising talent, she kept the company not only alive but in the black. Miss Sills is married to Peter B. Greenough, a direct descendant of John Alden.

*"I become poetic
tears may flow
when I think of my passion
for the Potato.
Over French Fried Potatoes
I really go ape
though Baked that are naked
are best for my shape.*

*And that Royal Potato
also known as dauphine
is enough to excite me—
just too too diveen.
But the yam of this recipe
gives me the chills
Try it, you'll love it!*
—BEVERLY SILLS"

YAMS/SWEET POTATOES

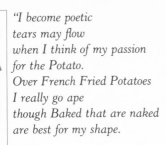

*Yams or sweet potatoes
Butter or margarine*

*Brown sugar
Raw cranberries*

Preheat the oven to 350°.

Peel and slice the yams to a thickness a little under 1 inch. Arrange the slices in a single layer at the bottom of a casserole. Top with chunks of butter or margarine over each slice and sprinkle brown sugar and a generous portion of raw cranberries over the layer. Repeat the procedure until the casserole is full.

Add enough water for 1 inch in the casserole. Cover and bake for about 45 minutes. Good with fowl, pork, and veal.

Mashed sweet potatoes—¹/₂ cup—has 13.0 mg of beta-carotene, slightly more than carrots and three times as much as spinach and butternut squash. New findings indicate that populations that eat a lot of foods rich in beta-carotene have a lower risk of developing several kinds of cancer, including cancer of the lung, mouth, throat, stomach, and colon.

LIZ SMITH

IZ Smith is nationally known as a syndicated gossip columnist and television personality. However, her friends know her as the "Potato Chip Queen"—almost unable to watch television or read without dipping into a bag or bowl of chips.

"My darling mother didn't care for potatoes, so we didn't always have them when I was growing up in Texas. But when she decided to make them, no one could beat her escalloped or her mashed. However, as a result of such sensory deprivation, I grew up thinking of potatoes as an enormous treat and I still do. They are just about the perfect food, and I often eat a baked potato and nothing else and go to bed happy."

LIZ'S BAKED POTATO FAVORITE

Bake potatoes as usual. Remove from the oven when they're soft. Put up the oven to 425°. Cut the potatoes in half, scoop out the insides into a baking dish. Put butter, salt, and pepper into the empty halves and slam them back into the oven to crisp.

Mash the potato innards in the usual way and reheat. "This makes two dishes and I can't ever decide which one I like best."

HEETE BLIKSUN

or Hot Lightning (from my friend Diane Judge's Dutch grandmother)

Poach potatoes, onions, and apples.

Rice them. Whip them with as much butter as your cholesterol count will allow.

Variation: Use carrots instead of apples and add a touch of nutmeg.

To bake a potato in a microwave oven, pierce it with a fork, place it on a paper towel in the oven. Cook on high in a 650 to 700-watt oven for 4 to 6 minutes, turning once. Let stand for 2 minutes. In a smaller oven, cook for 6 to 8 minutes.

Old-fashioned remedy to clear up tired, bloodshot eyes—slices of raw potato.

SUSAN L. Taylor, editor-in-chief of *Essence* magazine and vice-president of Essence Communications, Inc., is a national African-American spokeswoman. Her monthly column, "In the Spirit," her extensive travels, and her public appearances have made her the embodiment of the woman her magazine represents. She is the recipient of a Women in Communications Matrix Award and an Honorary Doctorate of Humane Letters from Lincoln University.

LOVE POTATOES

MAKES 8 SIDE-DISH SERVINGS

3 large potatoes, preferably Idaho
¹/₂ teaspoon ground black pepper
1 cup grated Parmesan cheese
1 cup grated Gouda cheese

1 tablespoon chopped fresh parsley
1 cup heavy cream
2 tablespoons butter, cut into small pieces

Preheat the oven to 375°. Lightly grease a 13 × 9-inch baking pan.

Peel the potatoes. Using a slicer or sharp knife cut them crosswise into thin (¹/₈ inch thick) slices. Layer a third of the potatoes in the pan; sprinkle with a third each of the pepper, the cheeses, and parsley. Repeat the layers twice, ending with parsley. Pour the cream over all and dot with the butter. Bake for 1 hour.

Note: To reduce fat and calories, substitute margarine for the butter and low-fat milk for the cream.

Additions to mashed potatoes: 1) Horseradish, or 2) a puree of black olives combined with virgin olive oil.

Variations on making mashed potatoes: 1) Bake instead of boil, 2) roast instead of boil, and 3) boil a mixture of water and milk before adding to mashed potatoes.

NO-RECIPE MICROWAVE
BAKED POTATO

"I don't have a potato recipe but I do have a thing about baked potatoes. To me, they are the number one comfort food, even more than chicken soup. If I have a head cold, I am happy just to have a baked potato and a cup of tea for dinner. If I don't have a head cold, I am still happy to have a baked potato for dinner. I just substitute coffee for the tea.

"Recently, I read in one of the magazines that I am served a baked potato in my office every day at lunch. Half of that is true. One year, my producer gave me a microwave for Christmas. Since I often bring my lunch to the office, I make myself a baked potato in the microwave. I bring the potato from home, carefully washed, since I like to eat the skin too. Then, when it is cooked, I douse

it with Worcestershire sauce. My father used to love Worcestershire sauce on French-fried potatoes, and the legacy continues. Besides, it's not fattening.

"P.S. After the baked potato lunch, I do the dishes.

"The restaurant that serves the best baked potato? I'm at a loss—so far, the best I've tasted has been in my office at lunch."

M R .   P O T A T O   H E A D

More than 50 million Mr. Potato Heads have been sold since his introduction in 1952. He met Mrs. Potato Head the following year and after a whirlwind courtship and brief honeymoon, they became conspicuous consumers, acquiring their own convertible, boat, trailer, airplane, and locomotive. They became proud parents in 1985 with the advent of Baby Potato Head. Two years later, Mr. Potato Head became the official "spokespud" of the American Cancer Society's Great American Smokeout. The Potato Head Kids now include Potato Puff, Lumpy, Dimples, and Spud. (Mr. Potato Head is a registered trademark of Playskool, Inc., a division of Hasbro, Inc.)

During the summer, vary an omelet by filling it with boiled and diced potatoes. Fold and refrigerate and serve cold, cut in wedges, as they do in Spain.

O one was more surprised than Dr. Ruth Westheimer when her academic credentials turned her into a media darling, known familiarly and internationally as "Dr. Ruth," a diminutive, dynamic advocate of "sexual literacy." And no one enjoys it more, delighting in it all. In this case, it really is *all*—radio, movie, and television appearances, commercials, a newspaper column, lectures, five books, and the board game called, what else, "Dr. Ruth's Game of Good Sex."

Born in Germany and raised in Switzerland and Israel, where she fought for that country's independence, Dr. Ruth studied psychology at the Sorbonne in Paris, arrived in the United States in 1956, and went on to earn a master's degree in Sociology and a doctorate in Education. While working with Planned Parenthood, she decided to increase her knowledge of human sexuality and studied at New York Hospital–Cornell Medical Center. The rest is history.

"Like most Europeans, I've always loved potatoes in all forms and shapes. The particular style that brings back the most memories is the potato latke, as that was always served at Hanukkah. We

would all sit around the kitchen table eating potato latkes, inviting in friends and neighbors. When I was ten, I was very fond of a little neighbor boy who was one year older than me. I can remember sharing latkes with him, and whenever I eat them now, it rekindles the feelings of those precious moments."

DR. RUTH WESTHEIMER'S BIG APPLE POTATO LATKES

("Courtesy my good friend Prof. Lou Lieberman, who not only is a sociologist, but a wonderful cook who's spent more time in my kitchen than I have!")

SERVES 4

4 cups coarsely grated potatoes
1/2 cup grated onions
3 eggs, beaten
1 large apple, minced
1 teaspoon kosher salt, or to taste
1/2 teaspoon pepper

1/4 cup matzoh meal
1/4 cup vegetable oil
1/4 cup butter
Sour cream or applesauce, better yet both
Cinnamon for sprinkling

Squeeze the excess water from the grated potatoes and onions. Mix the potatoes and onions with the beaten eggs, minced apple, salt, pepper, and matzoh meal. Let stand for 10 minutes to permit the matzoh meal to absorb some of the moisture. If still too moist, add another tablespoon of matzoh meal and wait for 3 more minutes.

Heat the oil and butter in a skillet and add the latke mixture. One serving spoonful will make one latke. Flatten the pancakes and fry until well browned on both sides. Drain well on paper towels and serve topped with applesauce, sour cream, or both, and a little cinnamon.

BASQUE POTATO SOUP

SERVES 6

1 pound chorizo or Italian sausage, sliced
$^1/_2$ cup chopped onion
2 (1-pound) cans tomatoes
4 Idaho potatoes, pared and diced (6 cups)
$^1/_4$ cup chopped parsley
1 cup diagonally sliced celery
2 tablespoons chopped celery leaves

$1^1/_2$ cups water
2 beef bouillon cubes
1 bay leaf
1 tablespoon salt
$^1/_2$ teaspoon dried leaf thyme
$^1/_4$ teaspoon pepper
1 tablespoon lemon juice

In a large saucepan or kettle, brown the sausage over medium heat. Add the onion and cook for 5 minutes. Add the remaining ingredients. Bring to a boil, reduce heat, and simmer uncovered for 40 minutes, or until the potatoes are tender.

BOB'S POTATO CREPES

MAKES 18

1 (8-ounce) package cream cheese, softened at
  room temperature
3 tablespoons flour
2 eggs
$^1/_2$ teaspoon salt
$^1/_2$ teaspoon coarse ground pepper
$1^1/_2$ cups (6 ounces) grated Swiss cheese
4 cups grated raw Idaho potatoes
3–6 tablespoons heavy cream
3–4 tablespoons chopped chives
$^1/_2$ cup chopped mushrooms, sautéed (optional)
Vegetable oil
Butter or margarine

Soften the cream cheese in a mixing bowl; add the flour and beat until smooth. Add the eggs, salt, and pepper; beat with an electric mixer. Stir in the Swiss cheese, potatoes, cream, chives, and mushrooms.

Lightly oil an electric skillet and heat to temperature just below that recommended for pancakes. When heated, add a small amount of butter and ladle the potato batter into the skillet to make crepes 3 inches in diameter and $^3/_4$ inch thick. Brown the crepes lightly on one side, about 3 minutes; turn and cook for another 3 minutes, or until the potatoes are tender. Repeat with the remaining batter, adding additional butter to the skillet if necessary.

If not served immediately, place the crepes on a baking sheet and reheat for 4 to 5 minutes in a 400° oven.

To freeze, separate crepes with plastic wrap and stack in a plastic bag. To serve, remove from the plastic wrap, place on a baking sheet, and heat in a 400° oven for 8 to 10 minutes.

IDAHO POTATO SOUP WITH HERBED SOUR CREAM

SERVES 3

1$^1/_2$ tablespoons butter
2 medium Idaho potatoes, peeled and cut
  into chunks
2 medium onions, sliced
4 ribs celery, cut into pieces

Cold water
$^1/_2$ teaspoon salt
$^1/_2$ bay leaf
Milk

In a medium saucepan, melt the butter; sauté the potatoes, onions, and celery for 5 minutes. Do not brown. Add cold water to cover the mixture, salt, and bay leaf and cook until the potatoes are tender. Remove from heat and cool slightly. Remove bay leaf and discard.

Puree the potatoes and cooking liquid in a blender or food processor in batches and return to the pan. Bring to a simmer. Thin with milk to desired consistency. Top each serving with a dollop of Herbed Sour Cream.*

*HERBED SOUR CREAM

3 tablespoons sour cream
$^1/_4$ teaspoon minced parsley

$^1/_4$ teaspoon minced fresh thyme or
  $^1/_8$ teaspoon dried leaf thyme

Blend together all ingredients. Refrigerate until serving.

IDAHO POTATO CHOCOLATE CAKE

SERVES 12

½ cup milk
4 ounces (4 squares) semisweet chocolate
1 cup mashed Idaho potatoes
¾ cup unsalted butter, softened
1 cup sugar

1 teaspoon vanilla extract
2 cups cake flour
2 teaspoons baking powder
½ teaspoon salt
4 eggs, separated

Preheat the oven to 350°. Grease and flour a 9 × 13-inch baking pan.

In a small saucepan heat the milk to simmer. Add the chocolate; stir until it melts. Stir the milk mixture into the mashed potatoes. Cream the butter with ½ cup of sugar and the vanilla until light. Stir in the chocolate-potato mixture.

Sift together the cake flour, baking powder, and salt; add alternately with the beaten egg yolks to the potato mixture. Beat the egg whites with the remaining ½ cup of sugar to form a stiff meringue. Gently fold the meringue into the batter until no white streaks remain. Turn into the baking pan and bake for 35 to 40 minutes, or until the cake springs back when lightly touched. Let cool thoroughly in the pan. Spread with your favorite chocolate frosting.

A *popular Peruvian dish is riced potatoes mixed with ground beef, raisins, olives, and onions, fried in oil.*

HUEVOS RANCHEROS SPUDS

SERVES 1

1 (8-ounce) can stewed tomatoes, drained
$^1/_8$ teaspoon dried leaf oregano, crumbled
Few drops hot pepper sauce

1 (7-ounce) Idaho potato, baked
2 large eggs, poached
$^1/_4$ cup (1 ounce) shredded Cheddar cheese

In a small saucepan, combine the tomatoes, oregano, and hot pepper sauce, breaking up the tomatoes with the back of a spoon; heat to boiling.

Split the baked potato in half lengthwise with a fork. Top each half with a poached egg, the tomato mixture, and cheese.

The International Potato Center in Lima, Peru, has more than seventy wild potato species discovered by Carlos Ochoa, a Peruvian taxonomist. Mr. Ochoa's searches have taken him everywhere from the South American island that inspired Robinson Crusoe to Andean mountain peaks.

"Anyone who can't make a mashed potato has no business standing behind a stove." Chef Daniel Boulud, former executive chef at Le Cirque restaurant, New York.

According to Robert L. Mercer, president of the National Potato Promotion Board, about 65 percent of the 35 billion pounds of potatoes grown in the United States each year are processed.

SALMON POTATO STRATA

SERVES 8

1 (1-pound) can salmon, drained
1 medium onion, chopped (¹/₂ cup)
¹/₂ cup chopped celery
4 eggs
2 cups low-fat milk

1¹/₂ teaspoons salt
¹/₄ teaspoon dried dillweed
¹/₈ teaspoon pepper
4 medium Idaho potatoes (6 cups unpared
    and sliced)

Preheat the oven to 350°. Grease a 1¹/₂-quart baking dish.

In a large bowl, combine the salmon, onion, celery, eggs, milk, ¹/₂ teaspoon of salt, dill, and pepper; mix well. Cut the potatoes into thin slices. Place half of the potatoes in the baking dish. Sprinkle with ¹/₂ teaspoon of salt and spread half of the salmon mixture over the potatoes. Repeat with the remaining potatoes, salt, and salmon. Bake uncovered for 1¹/₄ hours, or until the potatoes are tender when pierced with a fork. Remove from the oven and let stand for 5 minutes before serving.

"What your analyst can't do for you, mashed potatoes can."—People *magazine*

Peeling removes about half a potato's fiber.

Canadian by birth and long-time transplanted New Yorker, Enid Nemy has written for the *New York Times* for more than twenty-five years. She wrote the theater column for some years, and her Sunday column, "New Yorkers, etc.," was one of the most popular in the paper. She now reports on subjects as diverse as life-styles and travel. Her eclectic range of friends and acquaintances—from the theatrical to the powerful, intellectual, and artistic—is reflected in the zesty diversity of *Hot Potatoes*, her first book.